The Joy Bringer

Other Writings by Walter Lanyon

Available through:
Mystics of the World
Eliot, Maine
www.mysticsoftheworld.com

The Joy Bringer

Walter C. Lanyon

The Joy Bringer

Mystics of the World First Edition 2015
Published by Mystics of the World
ISBN-13: 978-0692352168
ISBN-10: 0692352163

For information contact:
Mystics of the World
Eliot, Maine
www.mysticsoftheworld.com

Cover graphics by Margra Muirhead
Printed by CreateSpace
Available from Mystics of the World and
Amazon.com

ৎ ঌ

Walter C. Lanyon, 1887 – 1967
Originally published 1925

Contents

Forward

Dear Anybody:

Whoever you are, I am glad that you have this book, because I know by the time you get through reading it, you will be one of an ever-increasing army of Joy Bringers.

You will soon see that it is the easiest and most profitable thing in the world to be joyous, and suddenly your kingdom of heaven, harmony, will descend as from a cloud, and you will sit on the right hand of the Father.

I love you, dear anybody, and I salute you with, "Peace be unto you" — the password of a Joy Bringer.

When you take this One Power idea into your life, you will suddenly become a Joy Bringer, and your joy will be full. It will be pressed down and running over; it will be as gleeful as a bird in the spring sun. It will be contagious; it will be golden, and it will be full of song.

Chapter I

The Joy Bringer

Nothing greater could be said of you than that you are a *joy bringer*. It may not sound like a great title at first, but the more you look into it, you will see that it is the "open sesame" to everything because:

> "He anointeth my head with oil (joy);
> My cup runneth over."

Joy is the oil that saves the material machinery from grinding itself to pieces and burning up with friction. It is the healing and soothing balm that brings peace.

Nothing can hold out against the spontaneous overflow of a joyous life. All things give way before it; and the best part of it all is that it is a present possibility for you. You, too, can be a *joy bringer*. You do not have to wait even a day; you can start right now.

The business of being joyful is the business of God. The people of God are a people of joy. You have been saying for years that you are one of His people, but can you say that you have been joyous or joy-bringing?

No! You will have to admit that life as a whole had come to be very much like a never-ending arithmetic lesson, with only occasional spots of joy. The very thing that you wanted most was the rarest thing in the world, and yet you kept reading over and over that all good things are yours. You just did not have time to be joyous and glad, and so the very thing that would have made the wheels go round smoothly and save you and strengthened you for real service was with-held from the machinery of life's everyday grind.

About the first thought that comes to you is, "This is not for me; I could never be continuously joyous. I haven't the time; I have too much to do," and like the foolish virgins, you think to get along without oil, and your light goes out at the very moment when you need it most.

No matter how good you are, how much you read and study and repeat certain words, if you are not a joy bringer, you are working in the darkness. You may not like to admit this, but the fact is that if you believed absolutely in one Power, you would be continuously joyous.

Why not? Think it over. Starting with the one Power premise—you say it is good, it is beautiful, it is the cause of everything that you can desire, and that Power is not only willing but urging you to draw at the open fount whatsoever you have need of. It is pouring into your life infinitely more than you can possibly use. It is offering you full salvation. It is bringing you into the kingdom of heaven here and now. It is fulfilling your least desire. All this you say is in the one Power, and you claim to believe in it and then are not joyous.

We must be honest with ourselves first. If we are not happy and joyous, it is because we believe in two powers. We may deny this, but if we believe in one Power alone, we become satisfied that absolutely nothing can happen that is not caused by that one Power and that it is good.

"If your eye be single, then the whole body is full of light."

Get hold of this one Power idea and cling to it, and you will presently see it working in everything, not only in your own life but in the lives of others as well.

In the Book of Books, we are told that after the creation was completed God said, "Behold, it is very good." What are you going to do about it? If you can find anything bad or distressing, then you can find something that the Creator did not make. And what the Creator did not make is made by your own little intellect trying to copy the Divine.

Either you believe that there is but one Power and that good or you believe that there are two powers fighting each other constantly, and you are little better than the heathen who tries to win them over by sacrifice. The fact is that the heathen, in his worship, spares himself—makes a material sacrifice and has it over with—but the worshippers of the one Power, who in reality have half a dozen powers to appease, sacrifice themselves to the despotic belief. They are worse than the heathen.

"I know, but—"

I can hear a dozen protests. "What are you going to do about so-and-so and this and that and the other thing?"

Listen, this is what we are going to do: we are going to learn how to get out of it all, how to transform it all, how to help, and go gladly through the glorious day with a song of rejoicing and praise.

If you know the slightest thing about radio, you know that you have to tune in to the various stations in order to get en rapport with them and enjoy the music they are giving. Your mind is, after all, just a wonderful radio set, only it is always tuned in to some station or other, and generally, the aerial wires, instead of being high in the air, are dragging on the ground, and you are getting the lowest messages that are being sent. The wires of scandal or hatred or criticism are dropped low, and they are busy all the time. There is a perpetual concert going on. If you enjoy this sort of thing, you must suffer the consequences, for the radio set that you operate daily takes the receiver with it to the same level as the messages you are receiving.

The laws of Life are few and simple. Think them over:

"Judge not"

Remember that in order to see something wrong with the other fellow you have first to possess that quality in yourself. The law does not change. If you are a "stone caster," remember that you will receive your thirty pieces of silver for your day's work, and it shall draw interest to the last farthing.

"God is not mocked"

You cannot get by with a single thing. The judgment that you have rendered against another shall be returned to you tenfold, "pressed down and running over." Criticism, then, is about the most expensive commodity you ever handled in your life. The rate of interest is so high and it lasts so long.

Remember that you are also a sending station, and when you are sending out messages of evil, you are only sending out boomerangs that will someday find lodgment in your breast. This is the law of Love. It is impartial and impersonal.

What good is it to say you love God and believe in Him, when you fail to observe the first law: "Inasmuch as ye have done it unto one of these … ye have done it unto me." If you have criticized, hated, or tried to make miserable "one of these," you have done it unto God.

But reversing all this, suppose you tune in to the good things of life. You realize the one Power and abide in it; you see the Good, God in every man. You keep constantly fulfilling the law of Love to all of "these." What a glorious concert will come humming out of the Infinite to you. What a song of joy and gladness will be yours. Yes, what a wonderful reward; you shall be called the Bringer of Joy.

You cannot imagine the joy of suddenly coming into full power of the truth that in reality you do not need to think another evil thought. You are free from bondage of material thinking when you realize that "behold, it is very good." Why worry, why be anxious, why care? God said it was very good and He knows, no matter what your sense testimony tells you.

Just as soon as you recognize this Oneness, you become single of eye; you get so accustomed to seeing good that good comes to meet you, to greet you, and to make you glad.

Go into your ark and draw in after you all the worthwhile thoughts, and then have a flood and drown out all the criticism, hatred, lack, and sickness that has been infesting your garden and made it a Sodom and Gomorrah. You can do this. You can have the baptism of the Holy Spirit the moment you decide to take God at His word: "Behold, it is very good." You can, from that time on, see only good and rest assured it will be good.

How often have you heard of a child in the night mistaking a burglar for Santa Claus and how the burglar, for that time, was Santa Claus to the child? "As a man thinketh in his heart, so is he" is the truth. You become the pivotal point in your kingdom of heaven, and nothing that maketh a lie can abide there.

Start right now and eliminate all evil thinking from your life. It is surprising how easily it will fall away from you once you let go of it. Begin to seek diligently for the good, and you will find it everywhere. Why? Because another law is:

"Seek ye first the kingdom and all
these things shall be added unto you."

Note the word *seek*. When you begin seeking for good, you begin to have "all things added unto you." And no matter what your problem is, if you will determine from this moment that you are going to seek good—and only good—and see only good, you will find that among the good things will be the solution of your problem.

Know this: that any failure you may have in your demonstration is simply in proportion to your belief in two powers. You may not like to accept this, but it is the truth, and when you become single-minded as to good, you will also be able to say, "Behold, it is very good."

And listen—when you take this one Power idea into your life, you will suddenly become a Joy Bringer, and your joy will be full. It will be pressed down and running over; it will be as gleeful as a bird in the spring sun. It will be contagious; it will be golden, and it will be full of song.

Your coming will be the signal for all worry to depart; you will be the most sought-after person in the world, and your price shall be above rubies.

As the sun shines by no outside power, neither do you require help or assistance when you once come into your own. When you once realize that "the Father within me, he doeth the works" and that "the Father and I are one," there is set up in your life a never-dying fire, which emits light, health, joy, and everything that you can desire.

"Take with you words, and return unto Jehovah." Take words of joy, of gladness and faith, and return unto the Father within. Talk with Him until you become so filled with the spirit of service that you rise naturally and go about your Father's business, the business of spreading joy.

When you come to the one Power idea, you realize that instead of being the rose on the bush you are the life of the bush. The rose is merely an expression of yourself, and you have the power within to constantly renew and beautify the body. You can cast off the old leaves and flowers and bud forth anew in greater glory and beauty whenever you desire. You can renew your body and surroundings by renewing your thought. You can cast off the thought of age and limitations and let the youth eternal be made manifest in you. When you are single in your faith, you can do these things—when you drop off the dual power idea for the God-power.

Now that you are becoming a Joy Bringer, one of the joyous things you will have to do is to keep blooming. Make your life and body beautiful, see it beautiful and good, and it will not be long before the man in the street will tell you about it.

It's worth trying—there is nothing to be lost and everything to be gained.

Let us first say to our body and our lives, "Neither do I condemn you." Free yourself from self-condemnation, just as you are going to free others from it. You have made mistakes, but now you are going to stop all this and cut short the self-condemnation. You can do this when you take the one Power, Good, as your guide, for from that time on you will not function through the carnal channels of hate, criticism, etc., etc.

Have faith in God; have faith in yourself as the Son. Faith is the thing that makes life easy and beautiful, the faith of a little child, we are told. And why? Because the faith of a child is productive of results.

Chapter II

The Love Life

Do you realize the power of Love? Do you realize that such an abstract thing can cut through gates of brass; can crumble walls away; can melt prison bars? No, to most of us it is a quality closely akin to giving up everything and assuming a patient attitude of waiting for our demonstrations.

The reverse of this is the truth. Love is the great invisible armor which surrounds you and is perfect protection against the most wicked thrusts. It makes you absolutely safe against sudden attacks from the enemy; it makes it possible for you to "set yourself ... and see the salvation of the Lord."

Love seems to be invisible to most of us, yet it is the most visible thing in the world. It is constantly with us. If a gardener loves flowers, his love will be manifested in a great variety of blossoms. As his love increases, he will be more and more selective, seeking better manifestations of it. If a man loves books, he will draw beautiful and wonderfully bound volumes of master thoughts unto himself. If a man loves pictures, he will draw unto himself rare and beautiful masterpieces. If a man loves people, he shall draw unto himself thousands of souls ready to express or reflect back to him the thought which he is giving them. Thus we see that a man's love is reflected in all that is about him. Love is made manifest constantly in myriads of ways.

We all know the qualities of love. A life which has adopted it is not only forceful but noble, firm, and gentle. Once a man has decided to take on the love life, he suddenly finds his whole way lightened with a new illumination. His business is to *impart love.* Constantly thinking on ways and means of imparting love, his life naturally becomes lovely, for the thing we meditate upon becomes a part of our makeup. What, then, could be more wonderful than to start right this moment to live a love life? Right now, throw every bit of criticism, hatred, fear, revenge, and envy out. What a load of rubbish you have thrown over the cliff of oblivion, and how free and peaceful it seems to be rid of the thought of getting even with your enemies.

What a joy there is in the work that is done with *love*. "Love goes all the way; duty tires when half through." When we love our work, when we love the workers, when we love the day, the country, the town, the home that we have—when we love everything, then everything will love us, and we shall find ourselves already in the kingdom of heaven. We shall tread the magic way where flowers bloom at our coming. We shall find that one of the most joyous things in the world is the pursuit of the right kind of happiness, the happiness that comes from serving and helping others out of their difficulties.

When man is poised in love, he finds that his former failure was due to the fact that a large portion of his mind or thought was filled with fear, revenge, hatred, criticism. Now that he has gotten rid of these, his capacity is suddenly enlarged. The little plant inside the narrow confines of the seed has suddenly grown into a vigorous thing of glorious beauty. It has filled the whole space, and its perfume spreads everywhere. A love life is felt in all directions because it is a thing of shining beauty.

What does the love life give to a man? It connects him with an inexhaustible fountain that supplies him with the pure spirit of youth and fills him with fresh enthusiasm, with wondrous visions of what he may accomplish. It takes away the bugaboo called procrastination and puts in its place accomplishment. It brings to him his own, no matter where he is located. It fills his mind with the ease of perfect trusting and spreads about him the great peace which the world does not know. It brings him poise, balance, and power.

It causes him to realize that leading the love life is like connecting up a completely wired house with a power plant. Instantly, in any place or at any time, he can turn on the power. Instantly, he can connect up with the universal Mind, God, and find the exact answer to his problem; can draw continuously upon the inexhaustible ideas; can know that these ideas are constantly being supplied to him for his use.

Once a man has gotten into the habit of drawing upon the Father for ideas instead of things, he will find that the things just naturally take care of themselves. Ideas are the substance—the spiritual substance that is transformed though our thinking into tangible things—which becomes flesh and dwells among us. Jesus knew the idea *supply*, or *substance*, was with him, and so he drew on it for all the bread and fishes he wanted in a place where, to sense, neither was available. When man allies himself with God and knows that he is one with the Father within, then, and then only, can he appropriate the magnificent inheritance which is his as a son of God. Gradually he comes to understand the idea of body.

> "For we have many members in one body, and all members have not the same office: so we, being many, are one body in Christ, and every one members one of another."

We can, then, by looking into the idea *body*, find that we are all members of the body of Christ. That is, we are all part and parcel of the whole and are therefore fed, sustained, and supplied by the same River of Life which is flowing in the midst of the

Garden. We know also that as in the material body so in the spiritual—every member is of importance and is just as precious as any other. We know that in the material body the blood courses through the body in especially prepared channels, and there is not one part of the body where it is not carried in abundance, bringing nutriment and taking away impurities; so in the body of Christ, we find the lifestream of ideas circulating, supplying whatever the member is in need of.

We are not a separate and isolated idea but a member that is a part of the whole, and we cannot escape the influence of the Master when we realize that we are a part of His heavenly body and listen for the instructions which He gives us through "the still small voice."

When we realize that we are members of the body of Christ, we also realize that the still small voice which speaks to us is very much akin to the way we speak to our material bodies. For instance, if you see a book on a table across the room which you wish to read, you certainly direct your body to get it; yet you do not actually voice this thought in audible words. So it is with the Christ-body. You, as a member, are instructed, guided, and protected constantly, and by virtue of your position in this grand scheme of Life, you are constantly en rapport with Mind.

Think deeply about this wonderful truth. Think, then, how futile it is for you to struggle materially. Put on the love life; get the habit of imparting love. Live it, breathe it, sing it, and rejoice in it. Suddenly you have come to the realization that you are a member of the body of Christ, and that the magnificent Mind which was able to work through the man Jesus is now working through you, and that you do not have to worry or be anxious. You are a member of the one Body and you do not have to worry. You are dependent on the Christ-Mind which is at the head of the whole plan and which will direct you as a member of the one Body.

> Let nothing disturb thee,
>   Nothing affright thee;
>   All things are passing;
>   God never changeth.
> —Teresa de Ávila

God is your life, the thing that is worth-while and *all* that is worthwhile. Material things change, but the God which is your life never changes. Fear not, then. Get in harmony with the body of Christ; find your place by putting on the love life. *Impart love* and be at peace with the world and with God.

Chapter III

Binding Things in Heaven

That which you bind in heaven shall be loosed on the earth. This is a statement which stands wrapped in mystery to many people, and yet it contains one of the most perfect laws of metaphysics.

Starting with the correct definition of heaven, we find that it is not a locality but a state of right thinking. When we are thinking rightly, we are in the kingdom of heaven and can understand readily the statement, "The kingdom of heaven is at hand (it is within you)." Naturally, it follows that the Father, God, dwells in the kingdom of heaven, which means that He is always present in the right-thinking mind. From this we see that what we bind in right thinking—what we claim or decree in right thinking—shall be loosed on the earth; that is, shall be made flesh and dwell among us.

The same law is stated in, "That which is told in secret shall be called from the house tops." That which we decree in the secret place of the most High, that which we affirm as real and true, shall come forth as surely as the seed brings forth its blossom and fruit. "Be not deceived; God is not mocked: for whatsoever a man soweth, that shall he also reap." Whatsoever a man claims as real and true will produce results after its kind.

"Ye shall decree a thing, and it shall come to pass" is a law so little understood that it almost passes over our heads; it seems beyond us. We are afraid to take God at his word. We believe in what Jesus has to say but shy off when it comes to speaking with authority and to decreeing things. We rather feel that we are overstepping our rights; but there the promise stands, and only as we come out with a definite state of mind—a positive, authoritative state of mind which knows that right thinking is God in action—can we expect to demonstrate with scientific certainty the rules laid down in Divine Science.

Planting, planting every moment of the day, what wonder, then, the admonition "pray without ceasing" since prayer means right thinking. Some of the planting is mushrooms, some oak trees, some of it lilies, and some of it thistles, yet planting, planting goes on eternally.

Pray without ceasing. Start the process of right thinking and hold to it. Refuse to let wrong thinking have place or power. It becomes a splendid game to see how many times you can withhold weak, negative words and expressions and replace them with strong words of truth. It is great sport to see how many times in the day you have withheld a criticism, an unkind word or thought against another.

It is a joy to see how many times you can eliminate the thought of sickness, poverty, or error of any sort in your own consciousness or that of another by reversing the lie and claiming the allness of God. God is the life of man, for God is infinite Life, *all* life. Remember this and know that it is impossible for man to be sick unless God is sick.

Life is all there is to anyone. This is proven when the state called death overtakes a friend, for we know that the lifeless body is not that which we loved and respected. If we thought it was, we would preserve it like the ancient Egyptians did; we would not bury it but would set it up and worship at its shrine, as the more heathenish tribes of the South Seas sometimes do.

Life is the thing we love, the animating influence, the thing which is so infinitely bigger than body and so much more beautiful than matter. And we find that God is Life and that God is infinite; so Life is infinite, and being *one*, it could not suffer in part without suffering in its entirety. God cannot be sick, and "what God cannot do, man need not attempt."

Is there anything clearer than this—that in being sick, poor, or unhappy we are apparently doing something which the Creator of the heavens and earth cannot do. Let us then eliminate these beliefs from our consciousness, for there is nothing in Reality, Truth, to support them.

Remember that when you are going on a journey and get started on the wrong road, the best thing to do when you find it out is to go back and get on the right road. If you do this and continue to travel, you cannot fail to arrive at your destination.

Perhaps you have gone a long way down the wrong road, and perhaps the moment you reverse your course, a traveler comes by and picks you up in his high-powered car, and you are back at the starting point almost instantly. But perhaps you have gone down a selfish, personal, little road all of your own making, which is not mapped out for the general public and which you are blazing as you go along; then you may have to retrace slowly each wrong step.

Either way, whether fast or slow, whether you have assistance or have to walk alone, one sure thing is that you are bound to arrive, without the question of a doubt, if you will only persist in right thinking and doing.

And so in the morning before we arise, let us bind some of the sweet influences of life; let us bind them in heaven, the kingdom of right thinking, and during the day they shall be loosed on the earth.

For instance, let us bind the truth that "I shall see something good in everyone I meet today." This will not be a foolish optimism which is not practical; just try it and see. You go forth, and perhaps the first person you meet is one that you have a little grudge against. But wait a minute—today you are going to see something good about them, and so you are going to mentally see them without the grudge.

Do you know what this will do for you? It will make you a magnet; it will draw all men unto you because your consciousness is uplifted and uplifting. Letting the criticism out of your own mind, you fail to see anything to criticize in another, and having a fine, clean mind, you attract everyone to you, for everyone in the world is seeking light.

Bind thoughts of prosperity; have that comfortable feeling that you are provided for by an infinitely loving Father, that all is well. And bind close unto your heart that the lilies of the fields, that the ravens, that all other manifestations of His love are abundantly supplied, and a great comfortable feeling of peace and harmony shall be loosed on the earth, and also the substance of things hoped for will be manifested unto you.

When we bind the things in heaven at the beginning of the day, we find that the influence of it carries through the entire day. Every minute of it, we are so busy loosing this wonderful energy of good that we have no time to lapse into erroneous thinking.

Binding the love of good in heaven, we fail to have the usual interest in local and foreign gossip, in scandals, etc., and soon we find that those things are not mentioned to us so often, for we are so busy loosing the good on earth that we have no time to take in the details of some sordid life or some life of crime.

Bind love in heaven; see how quickly you can reverse the desired effect of some story of criticism. Say right in the face of slander, "Why, I find so-and-so a very bright person; they are clean, they help so-and-so," or something of that sort, for you can always think of something good, and it acts as an immediate silencer to evil. This method is certain death to the shafts of wrong thinking and is the loosing on earth of the things which you have bound in heaven.

When we bind love in heaven, we find it easy to set a watch upon our lips; we find it easy to practice the rule of saying nothing in the absence of people that we would not say in their presence.

We find that binding clean thoughts in heaven enables us to loose clean conversation on the earth. It purifies the language of a man. It rids him of the superfluous words of gush or slang. It rids him of profanity and makes his speech eloquent. These are some of the glorious things which are loosed on earth when we have bound them in heaven.

Chapter IV

You Are a Child of the King

All of us can recall some story of childhood by which we were indelibly impressed with the nobility of the king. With few exceptions, the kings of the make-believe world were men of great valor, men of great deeds, and best of all, men of great love. There was something in the king which instantly drew a line between him and the commoner—it was his nobility, his graciousness of bearing, his courteousness.

All these earthly kings and storybook kings emulate, in some degree, phases of the only King—Jehovah. All of them have one of His qualities, that is, power; some of them have many others, and all of them have nobility.

In legend and in history, we see the brave knight setting forth to overcome obstacles; his destination, the Holy Grail. It was his business to be an exponent of nobility, to be gracious, kind, and helpful. These are the things that marked him. Though he finally was reduced to rags, he still kept his nobility. Upon his breast, near his heart, might well have rested a single word, gold-encrusted and shining, a single word which would keep him noble as long as he remembered and used it, and he would remain a fit associate for king, prince, or layman. And that word is *love*.

How often we read of the doings of court, the excitement of some new presenter, the anxiety and fear of the would-be courtier, the arrogance and stiff-necked conduct of those who wish to win favor; but ofttimes, though they bear a title and are rich as a Croesus, they fail to give the impression of true nobility because of the absence of the keynote, the password, *love*.

Heaven and earth may become one by way of the great white clouds that tumble and toss about in the sapphire and catch in the billows of cherry blossoms, reaching up from earth in the spring. So a man may become one with the King of kings by putting on love.

When a man puts on love, he suddenly becomes conscious of his real Self—his real, sweet, worthwhile character—which has been besmeared with wrong thinking for generations and has suddenly come to the surface. It is a glorious awakening. He realizes that all that is worthwhile is his forever and that he is giving up nothing real; he is just ridding himself of a lot of excess baggage, such as fear, criticism, hatred, and belief in place and power.

Drummond has said in so many words that *love* is the supreme good. You that seek to be noble, heed this—you do not need to go further in search of good, if you only stop for a moment and realize that *love* is the supreme good of the universe. The wisdom of St. Paul caused him to say, "Now abideth faith, hope, love, but the greatest of these is love."

When a man puts on love, life becomes extremely simple; life becomes extremely harmonious; the music of the spheres is the rhythm of his own soul, and he wonders how he could have lived in the selfsame place and yet missed all the glories that are about him.

When a man puts on love, the eyes that have not seen suddenly receive their sight; the ears that have not heard suddenly receive their hearing. Tongues that have wagged and

said nothing or that have been cloven by fear
are suddenly made the instruments of a glorious strain of music that sweeps into a hymn
of praise.

Heaven comes down to earth. Man walks
untrammeled and free in a Garden of Eden,
into which no sin can enter. Man ceases his
labor, his seeking, his worry, and enters into
his true station in life as a son of the King.
From that moment on, he goes out into the
world with his badge of love glistening so
that others may take courage and heart and
live in the same way and become sons. He
appears unto the prodigal, the lost, and the
sick and bids them return unto their Father
the King—and lo, the sweetness of His holy
presence; He sees them afar off and goes to
meet them.

Think of it. The King comes to meet you,
the poor sinner, the poor troubled one. The
King comes to meet you with the robe and
the ring, and oh, the glory of that robe, with
its gold-encrusted word—*love.*

When this robe of *love* drops over you, it
shuts out the petty annoyances of the everyday
life—all the little fears, the little bitternesses,

the little griefs — and it puts courage into your heart, which is backed up by the words of the King: "The battle is not yours but God's (your Father's)."

Drummond has made a complete list of the qualities of love: "patience, kindness, generosity, humility, courtesy, unselfishness, good temper, guilelessness, sincerity."

Is it any wonder, then, that a person having these qualities is aristocratic or entitled to be classed under the head of nobility? Yet all these things are within your reach — yea, they are offered to you with the promise that they will bring deliverance from all human misery. Why? Because if God is the only Mind, then God is the only thinker, the only doer, the only actor, and He is backing up each one of the promises He has made to you.

Patience

If a man be patient, he has put away all sense of hurry, all sense of excitement, of anxiety. There need be no hurry, for all work to be performed is God's work, and He is working with you and can accomplish the work which is to be done easily and satisfactorily, without the element of time having the slightest thing to do with it. Somehow or other, when a man has true patience, suddenly the work is done and done well, without fatigue, without restlessness. He who makes haste usually lacks everything worthwhile. The King has plenty of time and plenty of help. Call upon Him; rest in the Lord. "Wait patiently on Love," and Love will find the way which is lost to you through impatience.

Kindness

Since half of our unkindness to our fellow-men is due to impatience, kindness is easier to grasp when we grasp the right conception of patience. Why be unkind? Ask yourself this question. It is because you do not understand God as all Goodness. God is kind to all His creatures, above the power of words to describe, above all that we ask or think, above all that we can imagine. We get pleasure out of being kind, and it is like throwing a boomerang, for it is sure to come back to us—laden with joy.

Generosity

Let the other fellow have his views. Remember that he has arrived at his conclusions through a process of thinking which has differed from yours. You would not quarrel with an acorn because it did not at once become an oak tree. Then have that same spirit of generosity with thy fellow man. Being generous rids one of many of the more noxious weeds of material thinking, such as jealousy, envy, and hatred. You cease your hatred, and instead of condemning people, you are tolerant, knowing the cause which moved them was not the truth. You root many lies out of your thinking by being generous.

Humility

Ah, there's the word. It is the quality that makes great men greater. It is the thing that unarms the most scathing criticism. It is the thing which unclamps the vicious grip of sin. Humility—it is a word breathed by the velvet lips of silence, a thing which prefers the good of another and in this very preference attains its own, without a struggle, without an effort, without a care.

Courtesy

In all things be courteous. Remember that no matter how appropriate some trite word may be, withhold it if it would not be courteous. Courtesy is a fine badge of nobility; it is the thing which lends splendid dignity to a man. It is a magnet that draws all men unto it because everyone knows that no matter what their case may be, they can bring it to you and be treated with courtesy. Surely, courtesy is worthwhile.

Unselfishness

There is no need for selfishness. The never-ending source of supply is pouring into your life as fast as you provide vessels to receive it. Nothing can stay it; therefore, there is no need to be selfish. Use, give, let go. Be a channel for Truth through which it may flow unceasingly to others.

Good Temper

We all know that a piece of steel is worthless when it loses its temper. The same thing is true of a man. There is nothing so weak as a display of temper. We know the substance of the proverb, "He that is able to hold his temper is able to take a city."

Guilelessness

In some way, the word *guile* has a slippery, sliding way about it, as if it were very closely related to the serpent. Be not beguiled into the narrow thought that Truth is difficult to find or that there is a group of enemies—such as animal magnetism, Catholicism, and malpractice—that can pounce upon you at any moment and that your only escape is to run to some person for help in order to rid yourself of something that does not exist. Just throw all that cargo overboard right now.

The only guile there is in any of these things is the fact that you have accepted as real something that is only a bugaboo and are suffering from it. But it is not real, so there is no need to fear it and nothing to put out and nothing to be overcome. I care not if a whole army were to malpractice on me, for as long as I know that such a power does not exist, I am free from its guile. God is the only thinker. Is there, then, any need of fear?

Be not beguiled into believing that truth is not universal and that every man on the face of the earth is not striving for it in his own way. Truth is everywhere, and everyone has a right to it, and everyone is seeing it in his present progress as best he can. There is no stereotyped way of attaining it.

Truth never has been trademarked. Truth is universal. It was here long before there was any means of setting up a press and making a brand or trademark for it, and it will be here after these things have passed away. Be not beguiled; be not a tool in the hands of this or that cause. Come out from among them and be ye free.

Sincerity

It is crystalline in its purity. It knows no deceit. It knows nothing out of the way to say about the party who has just left. It establishes a state of confidence in man that is above the price of rubies—cultivate it.

"Love never faileth." Think of it. When you put on *Love*, you can count on its standing right back of you, for Love never faileth.

> "Love suffereth long, and is kind;
> Love envieth not; love vaunteth not
> itself, is not puffed up;
> Doth not behave itself unseemly,
> seeketh not her own, is not easily
> provoked, thinketh no evil;

Rejoiceth not in iniquity, but rejoiceth in the truth;

Beareth all things, believeth all things, hopeth all things, endureth all things.

Love never faileth."

Love never faileth—make it yours today.

Chapter V

Be Not Discouraged

If you were working on a mathematical problem and came to the end of your process only to find you had made an error, you would know at once that you had not applied the principle correctly. You would not even so much as vaguely think the principle to be wrong. You would start over to solve the matter from the premise that the principle was absolutely correct, always has been and always will be, and that the problem could be worked out with ease when the principle was thoroughly understood.

When you fail to make a demonstration of Truth, what do you oftentimes say? "Well, I have tried and tried and been faithful, and for some reason or other, my problem does not work out." You are so busy with the problem itself that you have little or no time to go to the Principle, which you must abide by, and study it more closely and become more conversant with it. You spend all your time with the unsolved problem, hoping against hope that, after all, you can get through somehow.

In mathematics, you simply set aside the wrong results which were obtained through misapplication of the principle and go to work at the beginning again. Or if you are not sure about some line of work, you go to the principle of the thing and refresh yourself, then start out with the positive knowledge that if you apply the principle correctly, the answer follows without question.

If this is true in mathematics, it is infinitely more true in metaphysics. If it is true in solving the problems about material existence, it is infinitely true in solving *the* riddle of human life.

Note this one thing: until you are thoroughly convinced that you are working to demonstrate an absolute Principle that is always perfect and infallible, you are likely to whine around over unsolved problems, spending most of the time in failure, instead of going to the fountainhead and increasing your understanding of the principle.

Learn this: effect is not to be considered at all; seek only the causative side of existence. If a man offered you a loaf of bread or a handful of wheat, your human sense would seize the loaf of bread, but your wisdom would take the seed. Why? Because the loaf of bread, while it would more quickly satisfy human craving, would soon be gone. But the seed is the substance of increase and would grow into unlimited possibilities, for there is no end to the result of one seed if properly planted. In a short time, the result of one seed could make a girdle of flowers or wheat around the entire world.

You know all this—it is merely brought to your remembrance with admonition to "get understanding" and stop trying to gain material things. Once you have an understanding for the infinitude of substance, the material effect takes care of itself quite naturally. The harvest is plentiful; you can make it into flour and bread at will, or you can plant it again and increase the substance.

Keep your thoughts away from the seeming material existence and let them dwell in the kingdom of Reality. Remember that you are not controlled by the human being side of your nature, but the God-being side, which is the Soul, which is the Spirit that is one with the Father within and is a majority because of Its singleness. When a man begins to work on the inner side of his life, truly "the fields are white" with grain. A thousand ways open to him. Opportunity is not an evasive something but a sure thing, coming as often as man is ready to claim it.

Form the habit of first acknowledging the principle you are working with as absolutely above change and as infallible. This is your premise, so whenever you fail to work out a problem, do not give a moment's consideration to the failure. The only thing that is wrong is your application of the principle, so go quickly to this principle; seek a better under-standing of it and find out what you missed in your application and then work your problem out anew.

The day of the Absolute is dawning. We find arrayed against the Absolute those who are still making concessions to a number of things. They claim to follow after truth, and yet they acknowledge its limits, and they are mixing personal and human sense with it to such an extent that they prate loudly about certain kinds of truth—as if there could be more than one Truth.

Be not deceived; follow after no man, no matter what light he may give forth. Accept the things which he sets before you that you are able to prove, but let the man alone. Rest assured, as soon as you break from personalities—whether it be teacher, practitioner, or friend—the sooner you will find you are dwelling with a God-inspired race of people.

Pygmy personalities fade out; they are nothing but the material mist. They set up long dissensions. They strangle truth by trying to make it conform to their little idea of it. They look up rules and regulations and try to decapitate truth if it does not conform to the way someone else has interpreted it. Stay away from the mind which distorts little words into particular meanings. Away with this child's play—you have bigger things on hand.

You must discern Truth more and more in your life and in the lives of others. Spend no time in trying to define error of any sort. If it is nothing but illusion, why waste a moment's time on it? Look for good in everything and everyone. Error is nothing to turn from. It is simply nothing, and hence, the way to overcome the sense of it is to fill the vacuum with something that does exist. This something is the knowledge of your God-being!

The deep things of Truth are coming to the light. We are beginning to make a distinction between the *I* and the man. Those who are awakening are beginning to realize what body is and what *I*, or Soul, is. There is little ambiguity to the one who is seeking the Absolute.

"Who did hinder you that you should not obey the truth?" Was it a personality, a person who is supposed to have a super intellect? Be not deceived again; go not back to your bondage. Learn to accept the truth as universal. Learn to get the "sermons in stones, and good in everything" which Shakespeare tells about.

Chapter VI

Prosperity

After we have come this far, we are still reluctant to turn the matter of hard, cold cash over to a mental process. There is something too uncertain, something which constantly reminds us that we must work it out "by the sweat of our brow." But the fact is that we must resolve the whole thing into the mental realm if we are to gain the financial freedom that we are seeking.

Going back a little in history, we find that what we today call dollars and cents were not known and that men traded work for something to eat and the Indians traded skins for manufactured goods. The state of Pennsylvania was purchased for a few skins that were not redeemable for much in actual dollars and cents.

Today we think a thing is worth so many dollars and cents, not stopping to realize that it is the mental valuation which we place on the dollars that makes the value of the thing we are buying. If you do not readily grasp this, just look at the present situation in the European money market. The Mark, for instance, is identical in size and shape or color of ink and quality of paper as it ever was, and yet today people in Germany know that the Mark is only worth a fraction of its former value. The Mark has not changed — it is the people's idea of values. And so it is with our dollar.

During the World War, it was a common thing to hear it said that a dollar would not buy much more than a quarter's worth in normal times, and yet, there was and is no scarcity of money; on the other hand, there is an ever increasing inflow of it from every mint. Is it not then strange that when the standard remains unchanged we should suddenly find it changing in value, at one time becoming scarce and at another time plentiful? Does it not resolve itself into the mental attitude back of it? The standard remains the same, and it is just what we, the people, determine it is worth that makes its value. Then dollars and cents, in reality, simply stand for a mental value.

Now then, if this be true, we know that our mental capacity is not limited. We are not shut off from thinking as much as we want, and it is through this simple little rule that we shall demonstrate prosperity. When we begin to realize that value is mental, then we also realize that we have access to the real "substance of things hoped for," through thinking, and we stop seeking the effect and look for the cause, which is mind. We begin to know that "as a man thinks, so is he" is a very trite and true saying in regard to his financial affairs, as well as everything else.

It would be well, then, for us to adopt a prosperous way of thinking right now. Never again allow yourself, for a single moment, to think poverty. Never again acknowledge a limited condition or state of affairs but realize that since the whole thing is mental, you have the power to bring into manifestation anything that you need or desire.

I do not mean to say that you can sit down and think a million dollars into your lap without an effort. In the first place, you cannot easily gain the million-dollar consciousness, so it is better to begin by placing yourself in a state of consciousness which you can more readily imagine yourself in. Once you have set about correcting the poverty thought, you will find that new and unthought of avenues of supply will open to you.

A person who spends minutes a day in meditation on abundance and then goes about his work thinking, "I cannot afford this or that because I am poor," or, "I do not see my supply," etc., etc., cannot expect to demonstrate that state of finance which he should have, because his negative thoughts offset the positive to such a degree that he repulses the very thing he would attract.

Once you have decided to take the stand of thinking prosperity and refusing to see poverty or limitation in anything, you will find that the battle is half won.

Furthermore, if we are going to eject the poverty idea from our minds in connection with our affairs, then we must also refuse to see it in the affairs of others; we must absolutely fail to acknowledge it as a real condition for anyone. This will not make you stony-hearted towards your fellow man when he seems to be in need, but it will enable you to look on the suffering of poverty in its true light—as ignorance of God-given rights.

In the beginning—or before that, let us say—everything was evolved from formless substance, or Mind, which was brought into expression. Even the silver of your dollar was a mental thing at that time, for there was nothing but God, Mind. Then this Mind set about creating the different things in the universe; it pressed out, or expressed Itself in various things. So today we begin to realize that the thing we are looking for is in Mind.

Now, it is happily possible for us to link ourselves with this one infinite Source of all things, for we are made in His image and likeness; we are sons and joint-heirs with the Christ; and a little later on, we find that "the Father within me, he doeth the works." It does not say the Father outside of us, but the Father, Mind, within us, He doeth the work. We have then but to turn within and make our connection with the Father, for Jesus said, "I and my Father are one."

Now we come to the realization that we are one with the Father, Mind, Creator; and being one with the Creator, we also can, with absolute certainty, bring out, express, or press out that which we can imagine, for if you can imagine a thing with clearness, you can bring it out with absolute certainty. But if doubt or fear takes possession of you, your demonstration will fail, for "let him who waivers expect nothing from the Lord."

It is the relative mind and not the Father within, or divine Mind, which fears; it conjures up all sorts of hideous phantoms to be afraid of. It is the thing which says to you: you must work and earn your bread "by the sweat of your brow"; it says to you that your earning capacity is so much a week and you cannot get more; it says to you that you cannot do the things which your inner Self knows you can do. Therefore, when this carnal or deceitful mind is at rest, it is possible to accomplish wondrous feats.

For instance, not long ago a young girl walked about the narrow ledge of an apartment house, several hundred feet above the ground, in her sleep—a thing she would not have attempted when awake. The relative mind was out of the way, and the divine Mind was in control. All things are possible to this divine Mind, and that is the Mind which we wish to let work within us, while it is the mortal mind which we wish to eliminate.

The unlimited power of the divine Mind will work in you when you have overcome this mortal or relative thinking and given yourself over to the Absolute. This is not a difficult thing to do, but it is a thing that requires diligent watching. Idle words or thoughts are little seeds that will develop into weeds that must be garnered or rooted up sooner or later.

Accumulated wrong thinking sometimes seems like a mountain before us as we attempt to say, "I am abundantly supplied with everything I need." But just the same, a large mountain can finally be moved away with a shovel if there is no other way of doing it. The cleansing process, however, is not as slow as our illustration, for once we have taken our stand and realize that we are right now in possession of infinite substance, recognizing that there is nothing but an erroneous belief to handle, we will soon see great masses of wrong thinking giving away and floating downstream and the clear, calm waters of Truth being revealed to us.

One of the master strokes in demonstration is silence. "Keep silent before me." And remember that to keep silent is like allowing a seed to remain in the ground until it has time to germinate and come to light. Tell no one, talk with no one, discuss the subject with no one. Work it out in the quiet of your own soul, and when it is time for its announcement to the world, it will be so evident that there will be no need of advertisement.

Chapter VII

Cause

Back of everything there is a cause. Whether we are considering the universe or a rubber ball, we recognize that there is a reason for its existence, a cause for its being; and going a step further, we realize that back of the myriads of things, back of the differing graduations of life, there must be one supreme and infinite Cause, which we call God. In other words, the whole plan of things had to be conceived, worked out, and brought forth by a single Cause.

Recognizing this simple truth, the most important thing to be done is to examine into the nature of the Cause of all things, God.

We know that God is infinite; hence, He could in no sense be personal or limited to personal form. We know that being formless and yet causative, He must be the Principle underlying and overlying all that is or ever will be, and we know that He is good.

A good cause, which is infinite, could only produce good as a natural result, and it is upon this truth that we establish the fact that the universe is already good and perfect since it emanated from a good and perfect Mind, which had no competition or opposition and which is infinite.

We know also that in order to be expressed there must have been action and that this action, partaking of the nature of the Mind back of it, must be perfect and eternal, harmonious and satisfying.

These are simple statements, yet they are fundamentals upon which man is able to regain his perfect state of being.

Man is able to demonstrate this wonderful truth in proportion to his ability to have faith. If he has faith that there is a God which is good and infinite, he can by small beginnings prove that this is absolutely true, and the greater his faith the grander and more perfect are his demonstrations, until he reaches the point where he will speak the word and it shall be so, as did Jesus.

He may start with a faith as small as a grain of mustard seed and move mountains.

Hold to the thought for a single day, "God is good, and there is nothing but God" and see if mountains of doubt and fear have not utterly fled before you. As the young faith becomes stronger, man dares to hope that life, after all, is a thing of joy, a glorious something that is so perfect and full of happiness that it lives and moves and has its entire being in the sunlight of Truth.

Man begins to realize that "according to thy faith be it unto you" is a vital truth. If we have faith in wrong conditions or adverse circumstances, medicines, etc., we can expect them to respond in accordance to the faith we put in them. It is a known fact that drugs and healing methods of a century ago would no more heal the same disease in this age than a stone cast into the river would float. Why? Because faith has been taken from them.

Christ's message to mankind was:

Have faith in God. Faith is the sub- stance of your very thinking; put yourself into it absolutely—you have nothing to lose and everything to gain. All things are accomplished by faith in absolute Good. There is power in the thought "good must prevail," because God is infinite and eternal and never fails.

When the disciples failed to heal the sick man, Jesus said, "Oh ye of little faith." He knew that the healing was possible if the faith was strong enough. In other words, He said that if our faith is perfect, there is absolutely nothing that cannot be accomplished by us.

Chapter VIII

For Lo, the Kingdom of Heaven Is at Hand

Though we have read that the kingdom of heaven is at hand, yet there are few who take the statement literally, and this is strange, too, for it is one of the few literal statements in the Bible. We are told expressly not to look in a locality for heaven but to realize that it is right here and now.

Let us take this premise, then, and see what a different outlook on life we have. Suddenly, when you begin to ponder this thing, you realize that right where you are, at this precise moment, you stand in the kingdom of heaven. You stand, you live, you move and breathe right now in a state, or kingdom, of perfect and absolute harmony. You do not have to go somewhere to find happiness, to find health, to find prosperity; you only have to awaken to the fact that you are in the kingdom of heaven and all these things are right here for you.

As a further proof that you are in the kingdom of heaven, I refer you to such passages of Scripture as "I and my Father are one," and, "the Father within me, he doeth the works." Now, the Father, God, is perfect Mind enthroned in heaven, in harmony, and where He is, where God is, there is heaven. You see, then, the futility of even making the slightest concession to material laws or to the last enemy, for there is nothing gained by dying; a man cannot die into heaven, but he can surely live into it.

Jesus realized that He was in the kingdom of heaven, and when He left, He did not die; He merely acknowledged the Absolute and was translated, as were others. Those who "walked with God," that is, came into the full realization of the presence of the kingdom of heaven, did not go through the experience called death. As matter is acknowledged even by material scientists to be but points of force, which can be translated back into its original mental condition, why should we not take advantage of this pleasant manner of ridding ourselves of the material concept of body, instead of thinking that it must be cast off like an old garment?

To the average man, death offers one means of ridding himself of the thing called body, but to the spiritual man, the new salvation makes it possible to ascend above it. Not in the sense of material measurement, but simply rising to a mental state where he sees everything perfect and harmonious, here and now, and recognizes that he is already in the kingdom of heaven. When he has reached this state, there is no need to dispose of matter, for the material concept has disappeared of its own self.

Starting, then, with the premise that we are *now*, this day, in the midst of the kingdom of heaven, we go out of the home in the morning looking for the manifestation of heaven, and the first person we meet is a cripple. No, he is not a cripple—he is an idea of God, as perfect as when he was created, but the mist that "watered the whole ground" has surrounded his material condition, bringing with it the ugly pictures of ignorance and misunderstanding. Now that you are a dweller in the kingdom of heaven, you can quickly realize that beyond the shadow of mist is the real man, perfect and eternal, and so in place of the apparent deformity, you see the perfect man. In place of a beggar, you see the bountifully supplied son of God. In place of ugliness, you see beauty.

It is a most wonderful experience, this taking possession of your new home, heaven. Literally accept your home as the kingdom of heaven, and all fretting and worrying will cease; all anxiety will disappear. There is nothing for us to fight against, for we are told that the battle is not ours but God's. There is nothing to carry, no weight of materiality, for we are told to lean on Him. There is nothing to be desired, for we are living close to the fountain of substance, which is pouring out more than we know how to accept.

Then we are lifted up in thought, and when we are lifted up, we shall draw all men unto us. It is possible, yea, it is the duty of every truth seeker to practice this lifting up process on his fellow men, and it is done by leaving him alone, except for the wonderful impersonal help you must give him by lifting yourself up into the present state of harmony that is yours as a dweller in the kingdom.

This is no mere idle theory; it is a present possibility. This is the kingdom which you have been seeking, this is the door through which you have striven to enter, and this is the sheepfold which offers you sure solace from all the pangs of the so-called flesh. Jesus says, "Behold, a new doctrine I give unto you." "The former things (thoughts) have passed away; all things become new," and "the former things shall not come to mind nor be remembered any more." They are blotted out forever—all the trials, all the tears and sorrows, all the failures and struggles—when you come to dwell in the kingdom.

It is the sudden opening to you of a door which has long been closed, obscured by the mist of ignorant thinking. Perhaps you have followed the line of reasoning that says you can think yourself out of your difficulties, but never have you come point-blank to the reasoning that this very old universe of ours is the kingdom of heaven and therefore we are already living in it, and when we are living in heaven, all things must be heavenly; all things must be harmonious.

And now we take the positive stand that we will henceforth and forevermore see nothing but the beauty, holiness, and happiness of heaven; we will look for it everywhere because it is present and to be found everywhere.

Remember that the door to heaven, harmony, stands open. It is the door of your consciousness. It is the door over which you have guard, and you shall determine what shall enter there; but the main point to remember about the door is that it is open and needs a porter, or a guard. If you leave your post of duty and allow the band of thieving material thoughts to come trooping in, you will find your kingdom an inharmonious place, full of misery and unhappiness, so "watch and pray" (think rightly), that your kingdom (consciousness) may be the kingdom of heaven(harmony).

Chapter IX

Take No Thought

One of the things which marks the Master's career with extraordinary merit is the abandon with which He gave himself up to right thinking. So complete was His faith, His understanding, that His attitude of mind might be typified as "take no thought."

It is pleasant when one comes to you and says, "I have made all arrangements for a day's outing, a vacation, an evening's entertainment, so take no thought about it." There is an abandon, a letting go, an I-do-not-have-to-bother attitude of mind, which is very refreshing.

There is a difference in carelessness and abandon. Abandon is that state which relaxes, lets go, and takes the promises of the Bible as true and good, as promises that will and can be fulfilled without much effort, physically speaking. When we are carefree, when we are joyous, we are, so to speak, "taking no thought," that is, we are not worrying or being anxious about the sense testimony.

This "taking no thought" attitude brings a glorious freedom, once you come to the place where you recognize that because God is infinite Mind He will do His thinking, and that your taking thought is going to avail you nothing— that by taking no thought (getting the mortal thought out of the way) you are tuning in with the Father within and will receive messages, instruction, guidance, protection, substance, and supply.

The proof of the "take no thought" attitude is clearly shown in the case of the widow, who took very much thought of the reality of matter, and of Elisha, who took no thought but who poured the oil from the cruse into everything that was ready to receive it.

Christ took no thought of provisions when He went out into the desert with the multitudes. If He had taken thought, a special corps of officers and men, cooks and waiters would have been necessary to attend their needs, but He took no thought of these things. He *knew* that in the precise form and at the precise moment that He needed it, would appear the thing that He wanted and the thing that He asked for. He therefore found it unnecessary to take much thought about material things.

Take no thought for the journey. "I am the truth, the life, and the way." What more could you ask?

Take no thought for tomorrow; for tomorrow is only a thought in itself, a man-made thought. With God, life is eternal, without measure or limit; there is nothing to stint on or deal out sparingly, as so many days, to man.

Take no thought of time; do not measure your life by so many years. Call to mind this: that man was never born, and this being true, it stands to reason that he has no age. He has not passed through conditions that were infantile; he has not passed through certain growing conditions that cumber mankind with laws of disease or fear. Man is and always has been eternally one with the Father. With this thought in mind, one throws off the thought of age and stops saying, "I am so many years old." One no longer checks up his age, for he begins to realize that he has passed through a series of pictures which are not unlike the changing scenes on the screen—constantly altering and flickering on and off but not affecting him (the screen) in the least.

There is a glorious something comes to you when you realize that you have cleaned out this futile and stupid thing called age. It is only a belief of mortal mind and has nothing whatsoever to do with man. Forget all about it, or better still, "take no thought."

Taking thought is like hoarding up the manna. It becomes sour, old, and useless. Why hoard old memories and dates, thoughts of the past, comparisons, and the like, when daily the new thoughts, fresh from the mind of God, are available for your use.

Someone has aptly said that when we take thought for things that we say do not exist, like disease, lack, sorrow, etc., it is like saying, "There is no water in this cloth, but I must wring it anyway." Surely if you knew there was no water in a garment, you would not wring it. Then if you know that there is no sickness, no sorrow, no lack, you do not have to put anything out or wring anything out, but rather you will have to fill up the empty place with something real, the substance of God.

In truth, we find that the main thing is to bring in the good and powerful thoughts, and they of themselves will crowd out the evil thoughts, or perhaps what we call evil thoughts are simply a vacuum, which we must fill with the God-thoughts.

All this brings more and more to our mind that our business is not examining the nature of evil but imbibing the quality called love—filling our lives with it, taking no thought about anything else—and surely when this state has been reached, we will find our souls dwelling in the courts of our Lord, in the many mansions (the various stages of progress of man from sense to soul).

If you wish to stop taking thought of error, you will stop discussing the seeming condition of it. You often hear one admit its unreality and then set out into a discussion of its various forms, with details about their difficulty in overcoming it; and all the while they do not realize that the subtle thing which they are trying to put out is laughing at them and mocking their feeble efforts from beneath its mask of seeming.

One might just as well try to put out consumption as to try to put out a "claim of consumption." It is the same in either case, for "what's in a name?" In either case it is wrong, for we do not have to put out something that does not exist, that has no reality, shape, or form. But we surely do have to stop taking thought of it, and when we do this, we take from it the only nourishment it has—the food of our thought. What we want to do is to begin affirming the truth about the condition, to fill our thought so full of the true condition that the other is just naturally eliminated—because it is only an illusion, having no real existence.

"Ye are gods, and all of you are the children of the most High." If you are gods, what business have you thinking mortal thoughts? If you are children of the most High, why worry about what mortal man can do unto you? You have only to turn in thought to God and realize that you are at this instant in the kingdom of heaven to dispel the mist which is obscuring your birthright from you.

There is nothing difficult about this. It only requires a little practice to make it a very easy thing to do. Soon you will begin to see that all the material pictures about you are only different intensities of the mist which "went up and watered the whole ground," but that it has not in any way effaced the true image, likeness, or idea of God. Just as the blood flows through your mortal body so divine ideas flow though the infinite Mind; ideas that supply richly all that is needful for man's happy, harmonious existence.

Again, "Now are we the sons of God." Do you still lack proof as to the type and nature of the thing called Mind, which is thinking through you and which obviates the necessity of your taking thought?

"Ye are the sons of the living God."

The God whose son you are is a *living God* and is infinite. Then take no thought of life, for Life, God, will take care of Itself. Taking thought of life also brings into consideration its opposite, death, so take no thought.

Listen, then, what God has done for you. "For God hath not given us the spirit of fear;

but of power, and of love, and of a sound mind."

The gift of power is yours. You do not have to think or worry about a material counterfeit of this one Power, which is yours, for there is nothing material that can cope with it in any way. This wonderful power is *yours*, so take no thought of fear about material power and what it might do to you, for there is no such a thing; it is only a thickened mist which presents itself in various shapes, trying to persuade you into believing that it is something. But remember always that the gift of power, direct from God to you, is yours.

Then is there any need to take thought of fear? Even if you should suddenly be attacked by the mystification of fear, you can listen and hear this Power speaking to you: "Fear thou not; for I am with thee; be not dismayed, for I am thy God."

There you have it. You are reminded that not only the gift of power is given you, but that the Giver is right there to back it up and to stand back of you.

Take no thought of fatigue or weariness, for "they that wait upon the Lord shall renew their strength ... they shall run, and not be weary; and they shall walk, and not faint." Remember, it says you have to wait upon the Lord, wait upon Mind to think; therefore, put yourself in the "take no thought" attitude so that you can hear the instructions for over-coming the mist which has seemingly bound you.

Then it says that you have the gift of *love*. That means that suddenly, when you realize that you have this gift, you have dissolved the mist of hatred, revenge, criticism, and all evil thinking. It means that once you become conscious of the gift of love, you go about imparting love.

Think, then, what a wonderful mission you have in life—that of *imparting love*. Practice it for one whole day. Go out and impart love to everything that lives, and in the evening you will be in harmony with the whole world. You cannot help it, for all the time you are imparting love, you are actually in the kingdom of heaven and experiencing real Love.

Take no thought, then, of anything material, but "whatsoever things are pure, whatsoever things are lovely, whatsoever things are of good report, think on these things."

Lastly, again I say, "Take no thought."

Chapter X

My Ways Are Not Your Ways

"My ways are not your ways, says the Lord; for as the heavens are high above the earth, so are my ways from your ways."

The ways of material thinking in contrast with *God-thinking* are such. Stand in the center of any railroad track and see the rails converge at no great distance. Stand at the end of a tunnel and see it dwindle away to a vanishing point of light. Look out and see the sun arise and the earth stationary and flat. A friend who sits beside you can throw his voice so that your ears say it comes from the next room. Taste is wholly dependent upon the sense of smell, and this, combined with sight, can play havoc with man's judgment.

Carrying it further, material senses can also produce and suffer from all sorts of untoward conditions, which are classed under the general caption of "ills of the flesh" and which it is heir to.

But man, when he hears the command "Arise and shine, for thy light has come," realizes that to his dark night has come a star, and that star is the vital truth that "my thoughts are not your thoughts, and my ways not your ways." At first, it is a vague statement, but gradually man begins to see what the difference is and how, by accepting this difference, he can change the face of the universe, as far as he is concerned.

Guided by the beam of this glorious star, man finds that the rays increase in intensity in proportion to his willingness to allow them to pass though him. He finds that the light is using him for a vehicle with which to express itself better. "God without man would be a nonentity." "I and the Father are one." "The Father within me, he doeth the works."

Man begins to realize in a mild degree that he is not a mortal something, a mortal being, or a human being, with limited and distorted senses which twist everything out of shape, but that he is a God-being, working consciously and intelligently with the light or intelligence which is now centering in his temple or body. "If the eye be single (if we realize the absolute *One*-ness of God), our whole body (temple) is full of light." If the temple is full of light, then we have the "seeing eye," which knows and corrects the so-called defects of the human being senses.

Man finds the command of "let there be light" a most delightful course to follow. It eliminates resistance or insistence. Man ceases to struggle; he finds he already possesses the very thing which he has desired, and now he is coming to a very powerful use of it.

Man's unity is now beginning to be apparent to him; he is *one* with God, one with this infinite Power, one with this Light and Truth. Further, man learns that the keynote of success in handling this power is absolute faith. By faith were all things accomplished that could possibly be thought of. By faith, all the so-called material laws are set aside as naught and the reality of the God-being brought out in harmony.

Simplicity is the keynote now. Man comes to the lesson, "Ask, and ye shall receive; knock, and it shall be opened unto you; seek, and you shall find." He is not ready for this, however, until he has arrived at the absolute faith stage so that when he affirms a thing, he knows that the prayer of affirmation sent forth stirs the waters of human thinking and causes a healing or demonstration to take place.

His faith presses on to understanding, and he comes to the place where "you shall decree a thing, and it shall come to pass." But he is not ready for the full benefit of this lesson until he has effaced self to such a point that he will not in the least way conflict with his fellow man. His decreeing shall have a good and reasonable reason to be, and he shall then stand firmly on his decree and he shall see it come to pass, for he is now working consciously and harmoniously with the Father within.

Man learns, then, that his main object in life is not to change anything material but that it is simply to correct the mistaken sense about the thing called material. You do not try to make the rails of the track spread apart as you look at them in the distance and explain that they do not meet, never can meet, and never have met. What you do is to convince the student that what seems to the sense to be real is a falsehood and that, in spite of appearances, the tracks do not meet; neither does the tunnel dwindle, nor the sun rise, nor is the world flat.

With this assurance, with this under-standing, man proceeds along his way, disre-garding what the senses say. The engineer, knowing the truth, rushes his engine into the tunnel, which to sense seems impossible. His eyes say that the opening at the other end is not large enough for a lead pencil to go through, but his knowledge says that as fast as he is ready for it, the opening will grow in size and that by the time he has reached the other end, the train will pass easily though. The fact which we all know is that the tunnel remains the same size and does not change; it is only the material vision of it, the faulty sense of vision which changes.

Taking this thought into the business world, when a man is confronted by what seems to be a massing together of evil, dis-honest thought, which tries to cut off the way by which he must pass; when he comes to a tunnel of demonstration through which he must pass, and the appearance is that the end is blocked and is too small for him to pass through easily—he must instantly apply his absolute knowledge that it is only a seeming condition. It has no reality, and that which appears to be a blockade of dishonest thought will melt away as he goes on with the assurance that Truth is a two-edged sword, turning in all directions, cutting off the head of every dishonest thought that tries to make itself heard.

He realizes that the human senses are always deceptive and that the "single eye" sees rightly and, although appearances may indicate dishonesty, that Truth is the reality and there is no obstruction in the way of perfect fulfillment.

What he works on, then, is not to widen the tunnel or separate the tracks but to correct his mental concept of them. Once this is done, his passage is assured; nothing can keep him from reaching his destination.

Likewise, in sickness we do not try to heal any disease or diseased organ but try to make the patient see that it is the mistaken sense of the thing which must be corrected; that in spite of appearances, he is in reality well and strong; and when you have convinced him that the rails of material reasoning do not meet in the distance but that they are ever separated by a like distance, then his correct thought will eliminate the wrong bodily condition.

Then as he goes on realizing the truth, as fast as he advances, all fear of a wreck vanishes because the rails on which he is traveling keep separating as he pushes forward. And to this is added another glorious thing, and that is that when man gets this concept of treating disease, he finds that the so-called appearances of disease are wiped entirely from his body, which has now become the "temple of the living God," full of light and peace and plenty. He sets about scraping off the material veneer of age and other illusions and sees a thing of beauty, white and glistening; a place whereunto all men are drawn.

Chapter XI

Your Enemy

Have you an enemy who has done you a great injustice? Did he snub you? Did he lie about you? Did he do a lot of things right while he was supposed to be governed by the truth? Has he made long speeches or raised a finger of rebuke when another spoke in language which he did not consider scientific and then in his own way acted a thousand times worse? And have you secretly cherished the thought that he would be punished? In fact, have you not rather rejoiced in the thought that justice would sometime overtake him? And in your thinking, have you not pictured justice as working out into some material difficulty?

If you have, you had better stop it right away quick! You had better rid your mind of the thought that there is anything awful that can overtake him if you do not want that awful thing to overtake you, for remember this: whatever you make a reality of for him first becomes a reality for you, and if you think that because of his hypocrisy he could be overcome with some malignant disease, then unconsciously you are giving power to a thing called disease, and it can from that moment attack you.

Yes, I know you do not hate him, that is, you do not want anything but justice done. He did you a great injustice. Yes, in every court in the land, they would say he did you a great injustice—that goes without saying. But do not bring into your own life the law which you wish to operate in his. If you recognize and acknowledge that the law of justice is sure to bring discord to your enemy, then how can you hope for the law of justice to bring anything else to you?

What I want to bring to your remembrance is that you cannot think evil for another and good for yourself! This would be a house divided against itself, and it would surely fall!

You must stick to singleness of purpose, singleness of thought, and singleness of idea. Acknowledge good, hold to it, and refuse to acknowledge even the appearance of evil, and just in the proportion that you do this will evil become a nonentity for you.

Once you realize the oneness of Mind, your eye becomes single and your whole body is full of light. This singleness of eye, or consciousness, is a glorious life. It is the *white* life that is clear as a crystal—spiritual, loving, joyous, and pure.

"I know only good; I see only good; I hear only good." When you are grounded on this basis, you will find that having acknowledged no evil laws operative for your enemy, no evil laws can operate from your enemy to you. You fear nothing. There is nothing to be avoided. You are a master. No person, place, time, or circumstance can in any way disturb you.

You move on, impelled by the single light which is constantly blazing forth. You are not concerned what so-and-so thinks, what so-and-so does or says. You are concerned only with yourself. You are not afraid of any situation, for having wiped out the law of punishment, you have wiped out a great fear that has been dormant within you.

There is nothing to fear. There is nothing to oppose. There is nothing to oppose with. There is nothing to be dismayed at.

There is no person that is greater or more important than you. You need not fear their manner, their position, or their power.

There is no power that is formed against you that shall prosper. Because you are at-one with the single-lighted Mind, you recognize nothing to fear, to harm, to oppose. You are so closely allied with good that evil does not come within the vista of your life.

But what are we to do—let them sin and not expect them to be punished?

Sin is ignorance, no matter what form it takes. Whether it be murder or whooping cough, it is all of the same mistaken quality called mortal thinking. It is ignorant in every way, and ignorance shall have its school master. You can recall the price of education, how you labored to acquire the alphabet, the multiplication tables, etc. Ignorance has its school master; that is enough. The school master will bring about the change in the easiest way possible and the best for all concerned. Yes, the school master will bring it about, so "fret not thyself." Adopt for your motto, "What is that to thee? Follow thou me."

Oh, take this unto yourself; say it over every time you are tempted to criticize, to offer suggestions, to rebuke, or to feel sick. Let it ring in your heart until you image forth the Christ, for it is His voice bidding you away from the mortal chaos. Listen to Him; obey Him.

Dearly beloved, "What is that to thee? Follow thou me." Resolve from this minute that you will make this a part of your life, and you will find it sweetening existence more than all sorts of justice that you might wish to see meted out.

Chapter XII

The Still Small Voice

We have heard much of the *still small voice*; we have heard much of the listening attitude, the receptive mode. We have all waited for that voice. We have all longed for it, and we have all sought for it, but in vain. It has not spoken. It has been the elusive thing which was fraught with uncertainty. No sooner did it speak, or we thought it spoke, than came the doubt as to whether it was the still small voice or the whisperings of mortal mind. And why has this been so evasive? We are told that it shall speak to us and say, "This is the way, go thou in it," or, "Turn to the right or left," etc., etc. Yet the promise has not been fulfilled so far as we are concerned. Why is this?

When you seek diligently, when you delve deep into mysteries, when you try to force it through long repetition, then you are displaying one of two things. Either there is an uncertainty that the voice does exist or else you fear that it will not find you (notice the word *fear*) and in your fear, you repeat formulas, you pray beseechingly, you beg the voice to speak. But the voice remains silent.

No voice is heard above the voice of fear and her twin sister, doubt. Prayer that is beseeching, that is repetition, that is fearful is of no avail. The very thing you wished to hear is speaking constantly, but with your effort to hear it, you are making so much mental noise that it cannot be heard.

This is not a theory, a play on words; it is the actual fact of the case. The denizen of mortal mind clamorings keeps up such a racket that there is no key of your mind in tune with the Divine.

We have a very clear example of this given to us today in the concrete. Take the radio: you may tune into one station or another by the slight adjusting of a little dial. Another instrument in the next room may be picking up a concert very inferior to the one you are receiving. Both of you have the same sets, the same apparatus, yet you are attuned differently. The operator turns the dial quietly and slowly, and suddenly a burst of glorious music fills the room; the quiet of the room is suddenly made vibrant with the music. With another slight turn, he can pick up another class of music, a lecture, or opera. Suddenly it dawns upon us that the very room which we live in is filled with a million voices, is crammed full of music, is packed tight with messages, but the operator of the instrument decides which of these shall have the floor.

It is interesting to note that without the aid of this little instrument we hear nothing of the music and harmony that is all about us, in our very homes. "Eye hath not seen, ear hath not heard, the glories that God has prepared for them that love the Lord."

Then, in our own case, we get precisely the station that we tune in with. If we tune in with Truth, we hear the vibrant message of strength, health, and happiness. If we cut in on the mortal mind strata we get the unhappiness, vice, and poverty of the world. Some of us get our tuning instruments locked so tight in one pitch that we cannot receive anything but the troubles of the world.

Such a person is a disciple of the tragedy of living. He will tell you that life is a tragedy, that man is on the hunt for man, that poverty is the wolf forever at the door, that all a man does is pass through successive stages of fear; and he can prove it to you, just as the man who tunes in to harmony can prove to you that all is harmony and happiness.

This wonderful instrument over which we are sole custodian, this wonderful receiving set which is ours, is not subject to the limitations of the radio but is open to unlimited possibilities.

We need but turn about, adjust the thinking, to be instantly in connection with the heavenly concert that we desire. When you find things going dead wrong, then you must first completely reverse the process. You must right yourself mentally, even though your receiving set is screaming error so loudly that the whole house hears it. You reverse the thing; you cut into a new circuit.

You will probably experience some confusion in coming from the utter extremity of error into harmony, but this is just a clearing away of the mental debris, and by setting your instrument to a higher level, presently, as the din of mortal mind dies away, a sweet strain of harmony will come to you. You will find that reversing the process is not a difficult thing to do.

Just take a commonsense attitude towards it, as you would in mathematics. Do not rehash and flay yourself mentally for half an hour. Having made a statement that the reverse of the lie is the truth, you are then open to back this argument up by, "You shall decree a thing, and it shall come to pass." Take the Bible at its word. The promises therein are all kept and fulfilled when we accept them at face value. Decree the thing; cast out the evil thought and decree, "This day shall you be with me in paradise." This very instant you are in Paradise, if you but decree it.

The fear-thought that a miracle or instantaneous demonstration could not take place with you is brushed aside just as you erase a wrong figure in mathematics. Just relax, let go, and accept God at His word. It is the most glorious feeling in the world. "Cast your burdens on the Lord," abandon yourself to His love, and just listen with a wide-awake mind, and the still small voice will not only speak to you but it will come unto you and be your teacher, your guide, your protector, and you can summon it instantly, in any place, at any time, and find out the right course to pursue.

Let us rejoice — the simplicity of Truth has come down to earth. No wonder Christ said, "Suffer little children to come unto me." He knew that their ears were not dull and that their minds were not filled with conjectures drawn from material conclusions. He knew that they accepted that which was told to them as a fact.

Have you ever thought of the child faith, how it begets according to its faith? Just recall how long Santa Claus remained a reality for you if you want to see an example of what faith will do, even on a purely material plane. Your parents told you there was a Santa Claus and that he was coming, and he never failed to come — and he continued to come until some other child told you or your curiosity got the better of you and you started reasoning things out and found out that it was impossible for him to come, and so he stopped coming.

Just as soon as you found out in your mind that there was no Santa Claus, just that soon did he stop coming. You were not intelligent enough to realize that Santa Claus was just the material name for the giver of gifts, that Santa was a reality. "No," you said, "impossible; it cannot be done," and so you destroyed your Santa.

This is the point: that so long as you have the absolute faith of the child, so long as you take God at His word and do not try to see how He can possibly do the things He promises—just that long are you going to be abundantly cared for in every way. Do not try to figure out how Santa Claus can come down the small chimney; do not try to figure out how he can cover the whole world and stop at every house in one night; for when you start to figuring these things out according to sense testimony, they instantly seem impossible.

Underlying it all is the fact that God has infinite ways to bless and help mankind that man knows nothing of, that he cannot dream of, and that, just as in the case of Santa, He visits all the houses because the spirit of Love and the Giver is infinite and fills all space and has infinite ways to provide, so that the universal Giver is everywhere present at all times.

This is the way it is with God. Little children do not doubt him, take Him at His word, accept His promises, turn about and just reverse the sense testimony, and do not wonder how, when, or where the truth is going to be manifested—just decree the thing and let it come to pass. When you have the childlike attitude, the pure faith of your thought will open up your connection with the still small voice, which in reality is very close at hand, for it is "the Father within you," with whom you are one and with whom you have constant contact, and you will hear the word spoken directly to you.

Gain simplicity. I entreat you to get away from creed, rules, and rituals, of ways and means, and just turn to His promises. With the attitude of "Father, I believe," just accept the beautiful promises just as you did the Santa Claus promise, and it shall be unto you according to your faith.

Whenever you seem to be in the swamp of despair, just "be still, and know that I am

God." Be still and know that God, absolute Good, is *All*. In this way, you will tune in with the Infinite, and you will hear the still small voice saying, "Ho, everyone that thirsteth, come you to the waters, and he that hath no money; come ye, buy, and eat; yea, come, buy wine and milk without money and without price."

Could anything be more wonderful; could any message be more pleasing; could any promise be sweeter? And remember that His promises are fulfilled; they are filled full of substance for you.

"Incline your ear." "Ye shall seek me and find me when you search for me with all your heart"—another promise. When you seek with the heart, it is with feeling and faith. It is not with the cold intellect of the brain or the reasoning of mortal mind. It is the simplicity and faith of the child.

Suppose you make a practice of getting in tune with the Infinite and letting your instrument stay set at that pitch. Get into the kingdom of heaven and stay in it. It is easy; it is simple; it is the present possibility of every right thinking person in the world, for right thinking is the kingdom of harmony, heaven, and nothing can keep you out as long as you think right. No doors are closed against you, but remember you must enter by the door.

And remember that the door to your mind is always open. If you are a careless door-keeper and do not keep watch, you cannot tell what vicious thoughts will creep in and crowd out the good. You cannot tell what vicious messages you may receive over your radio because you are not watching it carefully enough.

So be a doorkeeper who shows himself approved, and you will live and move and have your being right in paradise, here and now, and the glorious music of the *still small voice* will be your constant guide.

Chapter XIII

Why Weepest Thou?

Perhaps no question could have seemed more futile and unnecessary than "Woman, why weepest thou?"—spoken to a woman standing at the door of a tomb in which had rested the body of her Lord, for even the body had disappeared, and the impoverished material sense had nothing but the empty tomb to gaze upon.

"Woman, why weepest thou?" What have you lost? Is man material, and does the body represent all that there is of the idea of the one Mind?

"Woman, why weepest thou?" comes the question spoken by the still small voice. Why weepest thou, if you believe in God, in reality, in eternal life?

"Because they have taken my Lord away."

"Why seekest thou the living among the dead?" The voice again bids thought depart from its dense material mystification. Old thoughts that have been made flesh and dwelt among us for a long time have suddenly been downcast, and yet we stand weeping for their return.

"She knew not that it was Jesus." So blind with grief, so deadened by the crushing sense of material separation, she failed to see that the very voice that spoke to her was the voice of the one she sought in the tomb.

Standing without the narrow limits of material bondage, the Christ spoke to her, bearing a message to her which was the highest proof of life eternal, and yet she knew Him not.

And so today, you who stand at the tomb of someone who has dropped off the accumulated material thinking called body will hear again, "Why weepest thou?" and you will answer, "Because they have taken my loved one away; yes, they have taken him away, and I know not where they have laid him."

Again the voice, "Why weepest thou?" It is the voice of Him you seek in the tomb speaking to you, giving you the message of His supreme test: there is no death. There is but victory, for "death is swallowed up in victory."

You who are grieving at the door of some tomb, do not fail to grasp this glorious message. Do not fail to put away the tears of grief and be ready to answer the voice — "Why weepest thou?" — with an awakening joy that comes with the understanding that Life eternal has neither beginning nor ending and that it cannot and does not become extinct for a single moment.

The *still small voice* of your loved one, whose real life is eternal, one with God, is pleading with you to stop looking for the living among the dead.

If you will but heed this voice, will but turn away forever from the tomb, and will pluck out of your thinking the belief that anything has died, has been buried, or can remain in the narrow limits of mortal confines, then surely you will hear your name spoken in the sweetest, softest tones ever breathed, bringing with it the blessing of peace that passeth all understanding.

And then when she turned from the tomb, she heard the word, her name, "Mary." That was enough—Life had triumphed. And so when the blessed revelation comes to you that you have not laid your dead away but that your dead have been lifted up, have been freed, have dropped off an old garment—oh, then can you truly say, "Death is swallowed up in victory." Then can you rejoice that all things are subject unto you through your understanding of your oneness with God.

If the thought of death oppresses you, you can realize that man is instantly supplied with thoughts of life—that the two cannot occupy the mind at the same time. If you realize that Life is already perfect, not subject to change, decay, or limitations of any sort whatsoever, then you will fill in the vacuum of the death thought with the activity of Life Eternal. Instantly you have at your command the ability to think of God, and if you are thinking about God, you cannot entertain thoughts of death. If you do not entertain thoughts of death, death does not exist as a reality to you, to your beloved ones, to any-body.

"Why weepest thou?" Because you thought something had been taken from you, when in reality it has been loosed unto you in an infinitely greater capacity. Nothing that is good ever dies, so nothing has been lost. Nothing can be separated in the one Mind, so there can be no separation between you and your loved ones.

Chapter XIII

True Prayer

We often hear the remark, "I gave myself a treatment for this or that," "I want to demonstrate such and such," or, "I have worked so patiently to make that demonstration." All of which means that we are working for a material thing in a very material way. Perhaps we think that we are not, but surely we are, and it is small wonder that the results are so poor.

What a man does when he treats himself or treats another, in the truest sense of the word, is not to pray for something to come to pass, for everything that is worthwhile, good, and real has already come to pass—creation is already perfect and intact. What he should do when he treats is to bring his thoughts in line with the divine Mind, and when this is done for a single moment, the demonstration is as sure to follow as day follows night.

This is the point so often overlooked. We find teachers, practitioners, and healers trying to demonstrate things—never once taking cognizance that it is already demonstrated, that it is already here, and all we have to do when we treat is to get in line with it.

This thought gives treatment a radical and new impetus. It starts as the Master started, with gratitude for the thing already at hand. It acknowledges at the very outset that the results are already assured and perfect. It has in reality only one thing to do, and that is to get the thought en rapport with Truth—this is the mission of prayer. If a man treats for health, he will get much surer and better results if he will simply know that health is already perfect and that what he is going to do is to change his thought about it —replace the thought of sickness with the thought of health. Then he will get in touch with the real Life, and immediately his demonstration is completed in the flesh— "in earth as it is in heaven."

What a wonderful thing it is to know that when we sit down to a problem we can say, "Well, the first thing I have to be happy about is that this very problem is already worked out; the thing that I have to do is to put myself in line to receive it." Just think of it, dear reader: whatever your problem may be, it is already worked out right now and is only waiting for you to get your thought in tune with it. Isn't this a glorious and inspiring start for any problem that may come to you?

You are not getting rid of anything when you treat. So many people think they have something to get rid of. They have not. What they are suffering from is the lack of something, and that something is God—Life—heaven. When we begin treating by giving thanks that the problem is already worked out, we feel something push towards us mentally and fill in the vacuum that the so-called trouble seemed to fill.

What a jubilant thought, what a thanksgiving, to suddenly come to the understanding of "my problem is already worked out; my part is merely to clear away the mist and behold the Truth."

What a new zest—there is no fear of failure, for it is already done; no thought of possible mishaps. The way is straight, simple, and narrow. It leads straight to your destination; and joy of joys, we have already started in that direction because we know that the perfect destination is already set for us.

So, dear reader, your problem is worked out. Get busy, then, and put your thought in line with the Divine. Get busy harmonizing your thought with the God-thought, and you will find that the mist of wrong thinking which has obscured your perfect birthright from you is cleared away.

I shall call to your remembrance such things as these: "all that the Father hath is thine;" "ask, and ye shall receive;" "prove me, and see if I will not pour out a blessing"—and many other similar assurances.

God has been urging us to get in line with the true state of life, which is already perfect and eternal, which is already harmonious. He is urging us to turn from the mortal testimony of incompleteness and say, "It is done. I will now align myself with it."

You remember, when you were a child, how some of your arithmetic problems were stubborn and how much it helped when someone came along and worked them out for you and said, "Now go over them; get in line with correct thinking and then put them on your own paper correctly." That was a happy release from worry; and today, the divine Voice is speaking, telling you that your problems are worked out and all that you have to do is to get in line with this wonderful truth.

"A house divided against itself shall fall," and so a man who has divided his attention fifty-fifty between God and the appearances of matter will fail. If a man keeps his eyes constantly on the ground, he cannot see the stars; likewise, if a man keeps examining into his material condition, weighing, checking, taking note of everything, he cannot dwell much on the "it is done" of Spirit, for he is closing the channel.

When you begin to treat yourself, just think, "My problem is already worked out," and having taken this mental stand, you do not need to examine "my problem" all the time.

Perhaps a good illustration of how the attention or thought should be aligned on God would be that of a man looking through a tunnel to a patch of sun-lighted landscape on the other end. The man who knows how to treat correctly will keep his eyes fastened on the destination and will not go stumbling along trying to examine the rough walls of the tunnel and believing that at every step he is getting into a worse state. He will go buoyantly along, knowing that his problem is already solved, for he can see the solution at the other end of his way.

> And behind the dim unknown,
> Standeth God within the shadow,
> Keeping watch above His own.
>
> —James. R. Lowell

Remember: He has chosen you; He is responsible for you; and He is not a respecter of persons.

What you see the other man possess can also be yours, if you will know that God is impartial and that he bestows no favors upon individuals but offers the open fount to all.

But of all the wondrous things, the most wonderful is the knowledge that no matter where you are, no matter what your problem may be, there stands this one glorious thing: "The problem is already worked out—my business is to get in line with it."

To get in line means to fasten the thought, once and for always, on God as the perfect Principle of Life, operating through you and by you and around you.

What more can you want,
oh ye of little faith?

About the Author

Walter Lanyon was highly respected as a spiritual teacher of Truth. He traveled and lectured to capacity crowds all over the world, basing his lectures, as he said, "solely on the revelation of Jesus Christ."

At one point, he underwent a profound spiritual awakening, in which he felt "plain dumb with the wonder of the revelation." This enlightening experience "was enough to change everything in my life and open the doors of the heaven that Jesus spoke of as here and now. I know what it was. I lost my personality; it fell off of me like an old rag. It just wasn't the same anymore."

His prolific writings continue to be sought out for their timeless message, put forth in a simple, direct manner, and they have much to offer serious spiritual seekers.

Walter Clemow Lanyon was born in the U.S. on October 27, 1887, and he passed away in California on July 4, 1967.

58263096R00071

Made in the USA
Columbia, SC
18 May 2019